THE M TOOLBOX

MW01291801

TOOLBOX

PUBLICATION PLANNING

By

PETER KRUSE, MD, PHD

Website: http://www.webalice.it/morarokruse/

Edition 1.0

Cover layout and photo: Irene Livia

ISBN-13: 978-1544254180

ISBN-10: 1544254180

ABBREVIATIONS

AB	Advisory board
AE	Adverse event
CC	Clinical claims
CFR	Code of Federal Regulations
EMA	European Medicines Agency
EQUATOR	Enhancing the QUAlity and Transparency Of health Research
EU	European Union
FDA	Food and Drug Administration
GCP	Good clinical practice
GP	General practicioner
GPP	Good publication practice
HCP	Health care provider
HR	Human resources
ICH	Intl. Conference on Harmonization
ICMJE	Intl. Comm. of Medical Journal Editors

IICT	Investigator initiated clinical trial
ISO	Intl. Organization for Standardization
IVD	In vitro diagnostic
JCR	Journal Citation Reports
KOL	Key opinion leader
KPI	Key performance indicator
MA	Medical affairs
MOA	Mechanism of action
MSL	Medical science liaison
NDA	Non disclosure agreement
NICE	National Institute for Health and Clinical Research
PE	Pharmacoeconomic
PP	Publication planning
R&D	Research and development
ROI	Return on investment
SOP	Standard operating procedure
TOC	Table of contents
US	United States

INTRODUCTION

Medical Affairs (MA) is the important function in a healthcare company like a pharmaceutical or medical device company defined as *the bridge between the R&D and the commercial side of an organization. MA consists of a team of medical professionals that support the scientific understanding of the company's products following medical, ethical, regulatory and legal standards.*

When I wrote a brief introductory book to MA: *"Medical Affairs in the Healthcare Industry"[1]*, I quickly realized that the subject is big and demanding. A lot of different skills are needed to do a good job in Medical Affairs. Readers of my book reached out to me with questions on how to gain more information on the skills and tools needed to support Medical Affairs better. A picture began to form as to what tools were frequently requested and it became clear that we needed literature on these tools as a platform for increasing the quality of Medical Affairs. Therefore in this book The Medical Affairs Toolbox, we focus on the main tools we have in Medical Affairs, a significant one being Publication Planning. Tools that really support the Industry we work in and that provide added value through good scientific understanding of the products we in Medical Affairs and the rest of the organization represent: A strive towards Medical Affairs excellence. Publication Planning is a good example of a tool that is mastered by Medical Affairs and is the essence of bridging R&D/clinical and the commercial side of the organization providing the right clinical claims at the right time to the scientific world.

Publication Planning is not a "one size fits all" tool; it will obviously depend on the type of product you will be supporting. This book will walk you through some critical steps in how to set up a Publication Plan – the rest is up to you to mold according to your specific product needs.

Publication Planning conducted by the industry has been described as a tool to deceive the scientific community. Publication Planning is not only done by the industry as academic institutions also plan carefully what, how and when to publish their clinical data. It is the aim of this book to promote scientific and transparent Publication Planning regardless of who performs this planning.

A Publication Plan is a highly strategic activity that is critical for the success of a products life cycle performance. Publication Planning should follow good publication practice so that scientific and clinical research is reported in a complete, accurate, balanced and timely manner and following applicable laws and regulations. As Publication Planning requires multiple skills such as clinical, biostatistical, scientific, information retrieval and medical writing, this book may be of interest to a broad range of experts involved in such planning and development. You may be one of these experts already planning or you wish to set up a completely new publication plan for the first time.

The examples that are used in the book are completely imaginary with made up product names for educational purposes only.

Peter Kruse, MD, PhD, March 2017

Table of Contents

Legal Notes

The Medical Affairs Toolbox

Publication Planning

CHAPTER 1. PUBLICATION PLANNING & DEFINITIONS

- Why Publication Planning?
- Communication strategy
- Publication Plan
- Publication Strategy
- Publication

A new treatment developed in the healthcare industry regardless if it is a drug, biologic or a medical device will during its life cycle, from early R&D to market introduction and during the entire marketing period, generate published data from research. Data is likely to be generated and published by the company developing the product, however data may also be generated externally through for e.g. investigator driven clinical trials or pre-clinical studies. *Publication Planning (PP)* is the proactive effort to provide an overview of all pre-clinical and clinical data available for a healthcare product throughout the products life cycle; it consists of creating a plan outlining a time map of what data is available when and where it is going to be published. This publication plan is linked to the products publication strategy and to an overall communication plan.

PP has been criticized when conducted by the healthcare industry with ethical concerns as this could be regarded as a selling platform[2]. It has the potential consequence of undermining the medical literature[2]. PP is also done by many academic institutions to maximize their impact (factor) of the research that comes out of these excellent places. So when the industry wishes to do the same with the scientific and clinical data supporting their healthcare products it seems justifiable. The important thing to remember here is that regardless where PP is being done, it will adhere to the international ethical and quality guidelines described in Chapter 7. PP should not be and is not a commercially driven activity. Done correctly, either by academia or the industry, regardless, it may lead to better quality of how clinical data is published.

So why do we need PP? Well, if you did not plan anything (which sometimes may be seen in small companies) data will still be generated and published. However, by not planning when, what and where publications are to be available for the public, you may not be able to maximize the potential scientific impact of such publications. Often lack of planning may lead to: Wrong timing (e.g., clinical data presented after the data of a competitor), too much data in the same paper (e.g., in pivotal studies data is condensed into one paper instead of planning two or more papers each with its own clinical scope), papers with insufficient data (e.g., papers generated with data from one investigator in a multicenter study not leading to any clinical conclusion), papers of generally poor quality, and papers targeted at wrong journals or low impact factor journals. Proactive planning of what, when, and where new data is going to be published will minimize the risk of some of the issues mentioned above and in general increase quality of the publications that support the given healthcare product.

Here are some definitions that will align our understanding about PP:

A communication strategy: A company's high level strategy on gaining product adoption and usage through: Systematic, planned dissemination of key messages and data to appropriate target audiences at the optimum time using the most effective communication channels. As such, mostly a marketing tool that should guide more than define the publication strategy.

A publication strategy: Here the scope and rationale of the publication plan is outlined linking it to the overall product communication strategy.

A publication plan: The actual plan over all pre-clinical and clinical data available already or in the future with information on what, when and where new data is going to be available in a publication. The publication plan is typically "owned" by MA. Some companies might wish to only map data generated within the company; others may wish to include also externally generated data (from e.g., investigator driven studies).

A publication: Any written communication available to the public of pre-clinical or clinical data including papers, abstracts, e-publications, review papers, internet/websites, social media etc., related to a given healthcare product. Internal study reports or regulatory documents are not part of this definition.

Having a strong PP in place may provide:

- Awareness of the product development before the product enters the market
- A valid support of clinical claims (CC) on a products efficacy and safety
- A good alignment to the overall publication strategy and the communication strategy for a product
- Optimal timing of clinical messages
- Better targeting of clinical messages to specific audiences

- Better clinical trials done for the right purposes with the aim of providing quality clinical data
- Build a "feedback loop" to R&D and Clinical development if gaps in important CC are identified (see Chapter 8)
- Better response to competitor activities

But let me be honest: PP is an important but time consuming task that involves multiple departments in a healthcare company. A lot of information about what data is/will be available has to be there for a good PP and this will involve many of your colleagues (read more in Chapter 2 about involved departments).

CHAPTER 2. TEAM AND INVOLVED DEPARTMENTS

- The owners
- Medical Affairs
- R&D
- Clinical Development
- Marketing & other Commercial departments
- Other departments

As Medical Affairs by definition is the bridge between R&D and the Commercial side of an organization and as such it is typically the natural owner of the actual plan. In MA, the task is often one of the main duties of the Medical Director. PP is encouraged by the important guideline from the (third) Good Publication Practice Group (GPP3) for communicating company sponsored medical research[3]. In companies where MA is clearly separated from the commercial part of the organization, there is full compliance with the GPP3 stating that "commercial functions should not direct PP or development (of publications)"[3]. MA has the clinical expertise, it is not part of the commercial branch of the organization and has the clinical and publication ethics background to lead this planning. Since, as previously mentioned, a lot of coordination of information and input are needed from the other departments (R&D, Clinical, Medical Writing, Data management, Biostatistics etc.), good PP is indeed a team work as encouraged by GPP3[3]. Obviously the company size will matter so that smaller companies may decide to work with PP in smaller teams than described below. And the roles of the different departments may also differ, but here are some examples on how the involved departments may contribute to a good publication plan effort (see also models of PP in smaller companies, Chapter 10):

Medical Affairs: The MA Medical Director typically owns the publication plan. She/he will ensure that the information that needs to be gathered both internally and externally is available for the actual PP. Also, this is the person responsible for driving the PP meetings with colleagues from the other departments (as a minimum R&D and Clinical). The PP will through these meetings be coordinated with the Publication strategy and the overall Communication strategy. A culture where the departments generating the pre-clinical and clinical data automatically update the PP owner with information on status of for e.g., clinical trials and especially if there is expected to be any delays in publication dates (it .... sometimes...) is a good culture .... the job for the PP owner easier! The main challenge for the PP owner is indeed to generate such a culture of transparency and pro-activity. In order to provide the PP owner with some sort of formal oversight of all publications going out of the company, it may be a good idea to have a sign-off procedure in which the PP owner provides the final signature on such publications.

R&D: It is normally in R&D that all the bench testing and pre-clinical data is generated. In large companies there may be one or several scientists in R&D dedicated only to the product related to the PP. The persons that are able to collect the information from R&D and that understand the purpose of planning according to defined CC, would be a good choice for inviting to join the PP team. Obviously this department has a critical role in the pre-market phase of the PP. However, I have seen good PP efforts that included input from R&D throughout the life cycle of a product and here are some examples: To provide better understanding of a product's mechanism of action (MOA) in general or for e.g., in certain subgroups of patients, to test usability for medical devices, to provide pre-clinical data comparing different competitors (if relevant), and much more. In the early pre-ma[...] it may be a challenge for our colleagu[...]ort the PP. Get used to comments like: "We usually go to present data at these experimental conferences and publish in these specific journals – so there is no need to change that". And often they are right. However, it is here a good PP can challenge whether the chosen venues for publication of pre-clinical data are the best ones for the product and company according to the strategies in place. The important role of mediator is here the colleague from MA that may balance the needs from R&D with the need to support the pre-clinical claims or CC.

Clinical Development: The Clinical director responsible for the clinical development plan is a key member in the PP team. She/he will give important input to what data on the products clinical efficacy and safety will be ready for publication and when. Very important is that this person will have critical information on how the product being clinically tested is perceived by the physicians and patients during the clinical trials. Clinical development may have knowledge of clinical data being generated externally (such as investigator driven studies) and the progress of such trials: Important input to the PP. The culture gap between Clinical and Medical Affairs is usually not so great. Good collaboration is however needed for the success of a good PP. The Clinical director has as part of being responsible for the clinical protocols of the trials also the responsibility of the authorship agreements with the investigators. That generates often a lot of discussion both internally and externally. But with the help of a-priori defined authorship, based on criteria for authorship in contracts and with the good publication practice guidelines (see Chapter 7) this can often be solved in a constructive, transparent and correct way. Another very important PP role for the Clinical director is that this person is responsible for the time line of the clinical study report and the following publications. Sharing this information with the PP team is essential. The PP owner from MA needs to balance the wish from the investigators with the needs of the PP. Often such sparring is welcomed as many complex clinical trials tend to publish too much data in their first paper. Here the PP can actually help with suggestions on what clinical questions each of perhaps several papers may answer and suggest to split one large and confusing paper into several smaller but focused ones.

Marketing & other commercial departments: In general, Marketing and other commercial parts of the organization can participate in publication meetings for educational purposes only and should not take part in the PP process itself[3]. Along the same lines, such commercial departments should not review nor approve scientific or clinical publications to be in line with GPP3[3]. Other commercial departments such as Sales are not normally (and should not be) part of the PP process.

A Marketing manager that is product responsible is typically chosen as the representative from Marketing to attend PP meetings to be educated on what data is being published and what CC the published data will support. She/he has often good knowledge of who the target audience for a product is through extensive market research; this is especially important for a new product or a new product area that the company is not familiar with. This information will be beneficial to the PP process to determine where to reach the target audience to maximize the impact of your publications. Interesting and very different perceptions on what the actual target physician group is may occur between Clinical and Marketing. Again, MA as the PP owner may mediate here to ensure that the PP target group is well defined. Market research can also (sometimes) provide information on where the target group goes to update on clinical knowledge (which conferences, what symposia etc.). You could be surprised about where the supposed target group actually gets its clinical updates – this is not always obvious. For PP purposes this information is very helpful as you will wish to present your clinical data to a relevant audience.

Other departments and functions that may provide important input to the PP:

Medical Writing can be involved as part of the PP group to assist in "front loading" relevant activities. Medical writers are often spearheading the writing of the study protocol, the clinical study reports, and often also the abstracts and papers that will be sent to the scientific journals. If the medical writer is part of the PP, she/he will be able very early in the process (read: Before data is available) to think of how the papers are going to be written given the trial design and potential results thus potentially "front loading" such activities. Therefore, it is a good idea to involve and engage the Medical Writers in the PP.

Data Management is often not involved in PP. However, as with "front loading" of the Medical Writing activities, Data Management can be involved in the PP activities to set the expectations of what data is needed and especially how the output should be presented (tables, specific graphs etc.). Sometimes the involvement of the medical writer is enough as she/he will inform Data Management and align expectations according the PP.

Biostatistical experts are often used to discuss the data: "So now we have the data, what do they actually show? – What may we say from these results?". Bringing the Biostatistical expert to review the PP may sometimes provide some excellent feedback and be a way to realistically adjust the expectations to data to be generated in the future. Sometimes, what we wish to claim scientifically or clinically in the PP will not be provided from our clinical trials due to planned design of the studies. So the Biostatistician can challenge the PP by double checking the protocol designs to validate whether the different studies will actually provide the data we are aiming at. Perhaps not a permanent member of the PP group but definitely a good ad-hoc resource.

Health Economy is a specialty function that in larger companies may be found internally and in smaller ones may have to be an outsourced expert. In the context of PP the Health Economist may assist in assessing the early health economic claims. Critical reviews of early protocols and input to clinical endpoints that may assist in cost effectiveness assessments can be helpful if conducted by a good health economy expert. Towards the launch of a new healthcare product, health economic parameters could be used to build pricing and reimbursement rationales.

Medical Science Liaisons (MSL) have a true advantage over office based MA staff as they have the daily interaction with the key opinion leaders (KOL's). Also not to be underestimated, the MSL's have a thorough regional overview of clinical care in a therapeutic area. Through this field based interaction they will learn about competitors, current knowledge and state of the art treatment that may change how medicine in the near future is going to be practiced. Such knowledge is essential to have as input to the PP. In some companies there is a communication from the MSL's in the field to for e.g. the Medical Director providing her/him with this information. In some companies MSL's take part in the formal review of the PP to provide field based input.

MA also often conducts **Advisory Boards** (**AB**) where therapy area experts are invited to give valuable information and input/ideas to different aspects of the development of the healthcare product. The value of having direct access to the best physicians in a relevant area often representing different global regions and as such different standards of medical care should not be underestimated. A review of parts of or the entire PP by the AB members may generate some good and sometimes unexpected feedback ("have you thought about presenting the results of the primary endpoint this way? It could be a more relevant presentation from a clinical point of view"). Stimulating and recommended provided that the advisors have signed a non disclosure agreement (NDA) as PP contains product strategic information.

Publication Steering Committees are sometimes formed to plan the development of publications from a clinical trial. Typically the clinical physician from the sponsor responsible for the clinical trial may lead such a committee together with biostatisticians and members of the clinical trial steering committee. The work of the publication steering committee will be important for the PP. The sponsor clinician would have a critical role in ensuring that the PP is followed with regards to priority of journals and congresses etc.

CHAPTER 3. PUBLICATION STRATEGY AND LIFE CYCLE

- What is a good publication strategy?
- Data driven CC
- Timing is of essence
- Life cycle requirements

A good publication strategy is hard to define. Two identical healthcare products may require very different publication strategies depending on factors such as when the products were introduced to the market, clinical indications, competitive environment, etc. A good publication strategy will ensure that quality clinical data is available to be published at the right time to the right audience.

It is much easier to define an insufficient publication strategy. Here pre-clinical and clinical data is generated without any plan in place, data is not supporting CC, similar studies are repeated (with no added value), timing is sub-optimal with regards to the life cycle requirements, studies are non-conclusive due to inferior design or under

powering and much more. So the good
publication strategy should at least:

- Follow the overall communication strategy
- Define the relevant target groups (think big
  here: Not only KOL's, therapy experts, general
  practicioners (GP's) but also patient groups,
  and even political groups could be relevant)
- Map relevant venues/events (symposia,
  conferences, meetings etc.) that gives access
  to the relevant target groups
- Ensure quality pre-clinical and clinical data only
- Follow the products life cycle (each phase will
  have specific requirements)
- Provide an overview of competitors and
  support the needs defined by competitive
  intelligence (competitors might generate data
  that raises new hypothesis requiring
  "response" from your product)
- Ensure perfect timing (a good example is the
  launch of a new healthcare product or a new
  indication of an existing product: Is all required
  data available to maximize the impact of the
  launch?)
- Ensure that the CC are linked to valid clinical
  data
- Ensure that ethics, laws and regulations are
  followed

Data driven CC: An important part of the publication strategy is to ensure that the CC are data driven. For all healthcare products CC on *efficacy* or performance and on *safety* are the essential ones. "ActTwoX is a glaucoma treatment that provides 20% reduction in the intraocular pressure (as a surrogate endpoint) after 7 days of use at the recommended doses". "Medical device Z is safe when used for Y indication in Q target group with the most common adverse event (AE) (bleeding) occurring in less than 1/10000 patients".

No need to mention here that CC are heavily regulated to avoid false claims (which is also bad business ethics) and which has led to some major legal cases when such malpractice takes place. Under the US "False Claims Act" some substantial settlements have led to fines to healthcare companies up to several Billion USD[4]. It is obvious that one should not generate false claims of any kind regarding a healthcare product, you may think. However, if it was that obvious why do we see so many violations?

Consider the impact of false claims from a business outside the healthcare industry: A car maker could (falsely) claim that a normal car would safely function on ground as well as a submarine: "This car may also safely operate under water"? Absurd, yes. Dangerous, absolutely. Business ethics = 0. When healthcare products have misleading claims (like when a drug is being claimed effective for an indication without any supportive clinical data) you may end up in a similar situation as with the "submarine car". A good publication strategy will outline the CC and link them to valid pre-clinical or clinical data to ensure that the claims are not misleading.

Other types of claims to be supported by data will vary depending on the healthcare product, here are some examples:

Pharmaco-economic claims: This economic evaluation of healthcare products may use cost-minimization analysis, cost-benefit analysis, cost-effectiveness analysis or cost-utility analysis to support the product. These claims may be important to patient, physician, and to healthcare providers. However, recently the claims have become important on national levels to decide which drugs should be subsidized. The National Institute for Health and Clinical Research (NICE) uses cost-effectiveness in their recommendations on what treatments are appropriate to use in National Health Service[5]. Quality of life claims could be used as part of pharmaco-economic claims or as part of the clinical claims.

Compliance claims: A drug or biologic with a longer half-life that needs to be taken only once a day may provide better patient compliance. A medical device that has a simpler design (or even a simpler user interface) could increase patient compliance.

Usability claims: Especially medical device designs can increase the ease of which the devices are used by the patient of the operator. Well designed surgical devices can provide a better handling during the surgical procedure (and that could potentially be translated into better performance and safety). As an e.g., a device used by the patients who suffer from rheumatoid arthritis may be easier to operate than other devices on the market – here one could think of relevant data on usability supporting such a usability claim.

Pre-clinical claims: Non clinical claims supported by laboratory bench data that may or may not link to clinical efficacy or safety relevance. The pre-clinical claims could be used to describe a molecule, its affinity to receptors and to explain its mechanism of action. Also, pre-clinical claims can be used to provide head-to-head comparison of different treatment modalities (comparison of competitors) on a receptor level or regarding definition of MOA (how the product does work).

Timing is of essence: One of the key success factors of a good publication strategy and of its PP is to provide the right timing of publication of the available data. In the overall strategy there is a need to map when specific data is required – so generating a time line is essential. And this is not easy! When you are relying on clinical data to be ready to be published at a certain time you must have a good collaboration with your clinical development colleagues. Get a good understanding of the how well the clinical trials are performing: Planned enrolment vs. actual enrolment. Discuss with Clinical development if the clinical trials are on track and understand the Gantt charts (a type of graphical depiction of a project schedule) to plan where timing for data base release, statistics, reporting and article writing are planned. This will give a good overview of at least when the data in theory can be expected to be submitted for publication. And the plans rarely follow what happens in reality. So for the good PP strategy it is important to have some alternative publication options for optimized timing. Global or large national meetings could be important drivers of timing. If you planned to have clinical data ready to present in poster form and this data is not available due to delays in the clinical trial, perhaps publication of the protocol is a way to fill the gap and to generate awareness and interest; clinical trial designs may be of huge interest to the clinical community. Another alternative is to look for pre-clinical data or pharmaco-economic models to present.

Timing is always a challenge and one of the best ways to stay on track for the PP is to have a well functioning PP team. The members have to understand the importance of reporting any change of dates for expected data relevant to the plan back to the PP team. A good PP team works with the plan and thinks of alternative publications in case of delays.

Rushing publications to keep a time line can lead to bad quality and suboptimal clinical messaging. This goes for any science regardless of whether it originates from an academic institution or the healthcare industry. Large complex clinical trials generate a lot of data that often takes time to digest and understand: "What was the observed efficacy?" "Was this effect clinically relevant?"

"What was the safety profile?" "How about rare AE's?". The point here is to ensure that the data is understood to a certain level before publishing it. A good preparation is part of optimal timing. As an example, rushing a publication from a clinical trial before the Clinical Study Report is final is not always a good idea.

Regional requirements may also determine timing of publications. Here the regulatory timing can be of importance: When will the new healthcare product be available in the different global regions. It is rare to have products become globally available on the same day as the regional regulatory clocks are different. Different regions may also be sensitive to publications written in the local language. English is indeed the main scientific language however the impact of publications in Chinese for the Chinese speaking regions or in Italian for Italy, just as an example, should not be underestimated.

Life cycle requirements: One of the drivers of a publication strategy is the product life cycle. Each phase of the life cycle will generate different requirements for data and publications: Pre-launch, Launch, Entry period, Peak period, Potential label expansion, and Exit period (See Figure 1).

Figure 1. Publication plan phases during the product life cycle

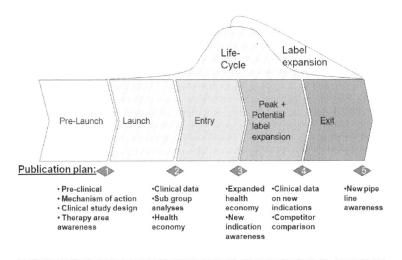

Each healthcare product will have its own life cycle and its own publication requirements. Below are just a few examples that may stimulate you and your PP team in designing your plan during the different stages of your products life cycle.

Pre-Launch: In the early pre-launch phase substantial clinical data may not be available yet. Especially completely new treatment modalities may require published data in the pre-launch phase to raise the clinical awareness of this new product. In the absence of clinical data, it is logical to present data from pre-clinical or bench research to, for example, explain the mechanism of action of a new treatment. Publications on the therapy area with quality literature reviews (systematic reviews) may be relevant to identify the existing medical needs or gaps in the current treatment – gaps where your new product may play a major future role. Such therapy area awareness papers should be published by KOL's in the specific area as they provide the therapy area expertise and credibility to this type of papers. Clinical study design publications have also both scientific and clinical merit in the pre-launch phase. Again "first-in-class" products may require new clinical study designs and new efficacy and safety endpoints. A good example is the introduction of (new) composite endpoints and the clinical relevance of these.The first available clinical data may be pharmacology and toxicology data that could be relevant to publish in the pre-launch phase too.

Launch: With a well prepared pre-launch phase where the new product has been well presented, the mechanism of action is known and the pivotal clinical study design is understood, the foundation of the launch will now depend on one thing: The clinical data from the pivotal trial/s on efficacy and safety of the new product to be launched. A lot of energy is typically and obviously put into deciding what to present and where to publish it at time of launch. What to present seems easy: "Just present all data from the pivotal trial" – however, that might not always be the most efficient strategy. Overloading the manuscript is easier than focusing it on a crisp and to the point presentation of the main clinical goals and results of the study. Often sub-group and post hoc analyses will blur the picture and may be much better presented in additional publications at a later point in time. A focused PP will help your company stay on track towards the pre-set goals of maximizing the impact of your product development. Inclusion of health economy data and results can sometimes be better in later publications if they do not serve the main goals of the clinical study. Where the first pivotal clinical data is published is very important. However, here the choice of the journal with the highest impact factor could lead to severe delays as these journals have high rejection rates. On the other hand, the main publication of the pivotal clinical trial is often the paper that will be the most cited one on your product and thus will gain the highest "impact factor". So some clever and strategic PP is required here. One common mistake is to have non-clinical experts in the therapy area to suggest a list of potential journals for the publication (for example scientific experts in the company that are not necessarily clinical experts). This could be a good question to discuss with members of your clinical advisory board: "What is the prioritized list of journals to submit our pivotal clinical trial data to, and what are the pros and cons?".

Entry phase towards peak: Here the scope is to expand the knowledge of the newly launched product. More clinical data from the pivotal trials could be relevant and now the post hoc and sub group analyses may become relevant knowing that the results are rarely conclusive but may be used in generating new hypotheses around the product. One typical subset of clinical data from the pivotal trials is to identify sub-groups of patients where trends towards better (or worse) efficacy can be identified. Such outcome may stimulate new research to focus on these subgroups and eventually could lead to label changes (broadening or narrowing of the intended patient population). During the period from entry towards the peak of the life cycle, expanded health economy studies may become relevant to "defend" pricing strategies of the product. Also during this phase some products may be considered for a label expansion sometimes identified via sub-group analyses from the pivotal trials. Some healthcare products may also be used in a very different clinical setting which will require new pivotal clinical trials to serve the regulatory needs. If the product is developed under the same brand, the same plan may be used. Alternatively, when using another brand for new indications, it is much simpler to generate a separate plan for the new brand. In the "maturation phase" from entry towards peak, competitor comparison may also be relevant: Head to head comparison of other similar products to identify clinical superiority with regards to efficacy or safety. In other settings, proving non-inferiority to competitors may be attractive if there are other factors that could show your product to be more competitive: Pricing, usability, compliance etc.

Exit phase: This phase may easily be forgotten as the products are not developed anymore and could be considered "cash cows" by the management. However, in PP it could make sense to plan for publications that would provide awareness to new products in the pipe line; this could be an overview of products in the same therapy area. Awareness papers can have clinical interest but should also be regarded relevant in branding your company as having expertise within a certain therapy area. An example of the PP activity in the exit phase could be: The glaucoma treatment ActTwoX is being phased out to be replaced by the better "first in class" new treatment ActThreeX – similar MOA, faster action and with a significantly better safety profile.

CHAPTER 4. PUBLICATION PLAN TEMPLATE

- One size does not fit all
- Publication planning drivers
- Key elements
- Rough template – an example

Let me begin by stating that there is not one way of designing a plan; one size does not fit all. The plan can be as simple as a table on a power point slide and much more advanced as a large report covering many facets of the PP process. It is in general advisable to make the plan as simple as possible to contain only the most relevant information needed for a good planning. The size of a plan is often depending on the complexity of the healthcare product. Advanced oncology biologics (like a monoclonal antibody) obviously will require a much more elaborated PP due to difference in target groups and in messaging when compared to a simple surgical medical device.

In this chapter we will look at some of the key elements in PP and will provide you with a basic template to inspire your build of a suitable plan.

PP Drivers: CC and clinical messages should be the drivers of the PP (See Chapter 8). CC generally describe something about your healthcare product. A claim has to be scientifically valid (data driven), fair and balanced to include both risks and benefits of the healthcare product; positive, neutral and negative data must be published in a transparent way. Definition of the CC for your plan is not easy and is often a collaboration between MA and Clinical. As Marketing does not actively participate in the PP process this department may still have important knowledge about for example new therapy areas; as such, input from this department on the CC could be helpful as part of fine tuning the CC. However, the final selection of the CC will be done by the PP team without any commercial influence.

There are obvious limitations to what you can claim depending on what data will be available and then there are important regulatory limitations that you need to fully understand before including CC in your PP. A review by your regulatory colleagues will be important here to ensure regulatory compliance. The exercise in defining CC will often result in identification of gaps between what you would like to claim about your healthcare product and what data you will actually generate through your clinical trials. These (important) gaps will often inspire the design of new clinical trials to provide additional clinical data.

Besides the product CC, the other key driver of the PP is the time line; as described in Chapter 3, the product life cycle will require a need for different data depending on what phase the product is in. So to simplify the PP drivers: CC and time line. The main scope of PP is therefore to define *what data to be available to cover what claims at what time line*.

The most basic plan could look as shown in Figure 2 with a listing of CC and main clinical messages related to a time line that may include major life cycle events such as "Launch" etc.

Figure 2. Simplified publication plan: Clinical claims vs. time line

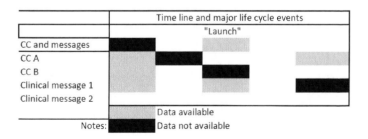

Each CC or key clinical message may appear on the time line with either a grey or a black box indicating *Grey*: The claim will have data support at the given time - or *Black*: The claim does not have planned data to support it and thus identifies a gap. Each box could in addition contain much more detailed information as *Key elements* of the PP as described below.

Key elements of the PP:

Time line: Keep the time line relevant and with a foreseeable future in mind; healthcare products, especially drugs and biologics, take many years to develop and for a PP to actually map the entire life cycle of a product not yet on the market could be an overkill (and a waste of valuable man-hours). That said, it is also important to keep in mind both the time it takes to design, execute and report large clinical trials; this is the time it takes to produce the needed data for your PP. So some planning ahead of time (2-4 years) will be needed with additional linking to major mile stones in the life cycle such as the Launch or a label expansion. Time that has already past could still be relevant to have as a placeholder in the plan to identify previous activity and which CC have already been covered.

Data sources and ID: Those sources are typically clinical trials that should each have a unique ID. Data could also be research from a data base or a patient registry. Additional sources could be systematic reviews, meta-analyses and other data not originating directly from company driven research. Firstly decide if you wish only to focus on internally generated data or you wish also to allow externally generated data (e.g., investigator driven research) to be entered into the plan. Keeping the plan to only include internal data makes the plan more simple and perhaps more precise as it is within your control. However, in some cases, it could be relevant to also include externally generated data sources. You may find relevant and much more detailed information on data sources in "Concluded or ongoing pre- and clinical trials" (see Chapter 5). In the grey box, identifying that you have data to present at the given time, you could write as an example:

- Data source name and ID number (e.g., GLAUcom-1001 if a study or e.g., IRIS-01-meta if a meta analysis)
- Title of manuscript/abstract/poster
- Keywords (1-3 keywords describing the key clinical messages in the data presentation)

Target journal (s): Here you prioritize the top 1-3 journals as target journals for the publication. Take into consideration what type of journals you are targeting and their typical review time. You should pull the data on target journals from the overview (see Chapter 5) and in the grey box you may include the following information:

- Name of the journals in a prioritized manner (e.g., 1. British Journal Ophthalmology, 2. Ophthalmology, 3. JAMA Ophthalmology).

Target congresses for abstracts/posters: A justified selection of relevant congresses should be made based on the information available in the "Meeting calendar" described in Chapter 5. In the grey box you may write:

- Congress/conference/meeting name
- Location and dates

Identified data gaps (only for black boxes): Here you present the gap between what data you need to present and what data at a given time is available. In the supportive information (Chapter 5) you have a gap analysis with more details about what data is needed and with solutions on how to fill these data gaps. In the black box you may write:

- Gap: E.g., Data on intraocular pressure with and without add-on treatment with carbonic anhydrase inhibitor
- Potential source for data: E.g., RCT comparing ActTwoX with and without add-on treatment with carbonic anhydrase inhibitor

Rough template – an example: An example of the simple PP with an "exploded" grey and black box with key elements information can be seen in Figure 3.

Figure 3. Rough publication template with time line and exploded grey/black box

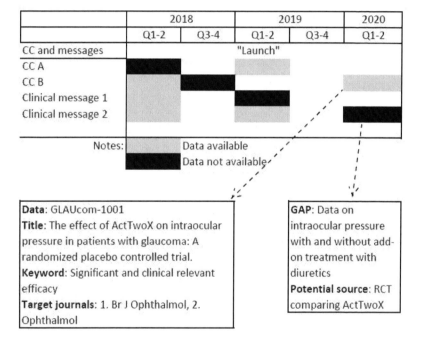

In addition to this simple plan it is important to understand that behind such a plan there has to be a lot of supportive information (the PP tools) that will guide the PP team in making prudent publication decisions. More details on the PP tools can be found in Chapter 5.

CHAPTER 5. PUBLICATION PLANNING TOOLS

- Clinical claims list
- Product bibliography
- Concluded pre- and clinical trials
- Planned pre- and clinical trials
- Meeting calendar
- Target journal overview
- Competitor overview
- Updated bibliography on competitors
- Ongoing competitor clinical trials

The supportive information needed to build and drive the PP is plentiful and should be regarded as important tools to have at hand when designing your products PP. It is highly recommended to have these tools ready <u>before</u> you write your plan and before having your first PP team meeting. You could consider each of the supportive information sheets as individual tasks that need to be presented in a simple overview for the review of the PP team members. You could ask each of the PP team members to take the responsibility to gather information for each of the tasks in preparation for the tools needed for the PP.

Needless to mention, you need to build in some sort of frequency intervals for updating the supportive information tools as the field of clinical and scientific publications is quickly changing.

Below is presented a brief presentation of these tasks that will eventually become the backbone of your products PP with some suggestions to who could take ownership of the individual tasks based on who may be best qualified. A multidisciplinary team will be needed to work on building these PP tools as several skills are required for the completion of these tools. Different sized companies may have to tackle these time consuming tasks with different in/outsourcing strategies (see Chapters 9 and 10).

CC list: Here you define your CC and key clinical messages that you wish to support your product. A relevant owner of this list is a colleague from MA. Marketing should be seen as a challenger to the claims process and should (as with other commercial departments) not be a part of the actual PP. Building your CC list is an iterative process where multiple reviews will be necessary to refine the claims and to adhere them to valid clinical and scientific data. Information on each could be:

- CC type: E.g., efficacy, safety, awareness, health-economic
- CC text
- CC priority: E.g., low, medium high priority
- Potential data support: Types of data to potentially support the CC, e.g., registry data, clinical data comparing X with Y etc.

You may wish to add different indications if your product has more than one indication. Furthermore, consider some kind of coding of your claims if you have many on the list, however, these codes are often more confusing than actually a help especially if you construct a plan as shown in Figure 3 where the entire claims are clearly written.

Product bibliography: This is an overview of all literature published representing your healthcare product. You may decide to include only publications based on internally generated data or also to include papers based on externally generated data to provide you with a broader overview (e.g., data from investigator driven research). In the early phases of R&D, the product scientist could be responsible for this task. Later in the products life cycle MA or for large projects Medical Writing could be responsible for the product bibliography updates to bring to the PP team.

The product bibliography could be divided into different indication areas if your product has different indications where keeping the bibliography as one could become too lengthy. However it will be the scope of the PP that will decide such a split of the publication plan into smaller ones. Also, consider to include both pre-clinical and clinical publications to give you a more complete overview of what is published. Each publication can be listed using a citation that is searchable in literature data bases for e.g., Pubmed or Embase or perhaps a specialty data base that serves your healthcare product better (e.g., PsycINFO, a specialty data base on behavioral sciences and mental health or TOXLINE covering the pharmacological and toxicological effects of drugs and other chemicals and many more). The basic information to enter in your product bibliography would be:

- Citation: Authors, title, journal, year, volume, pages
- Publication type: Original paper, review paper, meta-analysis, case story, editorial
- Brief abstract: Scope, design, results, conclusion
- Study ID: Provide the study number to identify which (internal) study the publication refers to

Concluded pre- and clinical trials: This is typically already done by R&D and Clinical and is a brief overview of all pre-clinical and clinical trials conducted by your company on the specific product. Typically such information can be found in the Investigators Brochure of a healthcare product. Here you may list the basic information of each concluded trial:

- Trial ID
- Completion date
- Title
- Brief design
- Brief results
- Conclusion
- Study report ID
- Planned publications and scope of publications

Planned pre- and clinical trials: As for the completed trials, the list of planned trials is always available through R&D and Clinical who may be the natural PP team members to own this task. The planned trials should be listed with brief information on:

- Trial ID
- Estimated completion date
- Title
- Brief design

- Planned publications according to protocol contract (if any)

Meeting calendar: An overview of congresses, meetings and conferences within the relevant clinical areas could be the responsibility of MA with input from R&D and Clinical. Marketing has expertise in where to identify target groups and as such may provide suggestive input on the importance of the different meetings. The meeting calendar can provide the PP team with relevant information of what important meetings take place, when, target groups, international/national impact, and specific focus topics of the meetings. To cover this the meeting calendar could include information on:

- Type of meeting
- Meeting title
- Target groups (type of specialists attending)
- Delegation size
- International/national attendance (estimates)
- Meeting dates (including dates for any "sub-meetings")
- Location
- Abstract deadline
- Meeting website
- Meeting frequency

Target journal overview: Each therapy area will have its target journals. In this book we have been looking at ophthalmology as an example and there the target journal would mainly be clinical journals within this therapy area but also perhaps some more scientific journals for the more basic science would be of interest. R&D and Clinical would typically give input to this list, however Medical Writing may have more experience with the bibliographic details that will be needed to list the target journals. This list will provide essential information about what target journals are relevant for the plan and perhaps also to what strategy to take in prioritizing journals.Here are some of the input that could be considered included in the target journal list:

- Therapeutic area (main)
- Title
- Scope of journal
- Circulation number
- Peer reviewed
- If supplement: Supplement peer reviewed?
- Impact factor (source: e.g., JCR[6])
- Journal web site
- Lead times: Submission-acceptance/ acceptance-Epub/ acceptance-paper
- Additional benefits: Possibility of publishing sounds, videos, pictures etc.

Updating the target journal list will obviously be critical as there will be new journals, changed impact factors, change in lead times and much more. Lead time is one very critical factor that significantly can impact your PP strategy. With new and fast online journals where the lead time is almost instant and where the accessibility can be very large, this should be taken into account when choosing target journals. Online publishing comes also with some unique benefits of allowing publication of sound, video, pictures and for peers to be able to comment online.

Competitor overview: Marketing will be the natural "owner" of the competitor overview and could be the driver of providing this task to the PP team. This involvement should not be considered as being an active role in the PP process but rather a resource for the PP team that will be responsible for the actual planning. The competitor overview could be divided in competitors on the market and potential competitors to enter the market. For the PP only basic information about competitors would be needed and the list could include:

- Labeled indication
- Type of competitor
- Brand name
- Company name

- Product website
- Importance ranking (e.g., low, medium, high)

Updated bibliography on competitors: Similar to having an overview of the literature published on your own product, this information is critical to have on your competitors too. Typical MA or Medical Writing could be responsible for such a task. It would be recommended to use the same layout as the bibliography of your own product and perhaps use a sort of ranking based on the "Competitor overview" mentioned above so you always can focus on the main competitors. Broad and good literature searches would be needed in data bases such as Medline/Pubmed[7], Embase[8], Cochrane[9], and perhaps other specialty data bases suitable for your product area. The input to the PP list could be (similar to your own product):

- Citation: Authors, title, journal, year, volume, pages
- Publication type: Original paper, review paper, meta-analysis, case story, editorial
- Brief abstract: Scope, design, results, conclusion
- Opportunity/threats: Highlight any opportunity or threats to your product

Ongoing competitor clinical trials: To be thorough and to ensure that you are following pipe line activity of your competitors (products in development and not already on the market) it is advisable to also follow the ongoing competitor clinical trials. This may be an activity for MA to be responsible for as part of the PP team tasks. The competitor clinical trials could be focused only on the main competitors defined in the "Competitor overview" mentioned above.

There are several clinical trial data bases you may search in, and here are two of the main data bases covering the US/EU regions: ClinicalTrials.gov[10], maintained by the US National Institute of Health and the EU Clinical Trials Register[11], maintained by the European Medicines Agency (EMA). The information that may be relevant for your PP is:

- Competitor brand name
- Study title
- Study scope
- Study design
- Estimated end of trial
- Opportunity/threats: Highlight any opportunity or threat to your product

This activity could be very valuable as a strategic input to your PP especially if the potential opportunities and threats are thoroughly defined and understood.

Chapter 6. Publication Planning Meetings

- Preparing for the first meeting
- Provide a PP tool template
- Who to invite
- Agenda
- Gap analysis
- Updates for next meeting
- Meeting frequency

The leader of the PP may in most cases be the Clinician working in MA. Why? Being the therapy area expert, scientifically trained, and the "bridge between science and commercial" she/he has the best skills and overview to assist the PP process in the balance between CC vs. scientific data.

In preparation for your first PP meeting you have defined the PP tools to be prepared before the actual meeting (see Chapter 5) and you have prepared the PP plan as a skeleton template only (as you will need the PP team input to complete it). The task of preparing the PP tools need to be well defined to each PP member.

Note that some of these tasks are quite time consuming; competitor overview, literature searches, just to mention a few, may require months of concentrated work to complete. It is worthwhile waiting for these tasks to be at least 80% completed before you begin PP to avoid a GIGO scenario ("garbage in – garbage out"): The entire PP is only as good as the input given to it.

You may be surprised that a lot of the information already exists somewhere in your organization – you just have to spot it and incorporate it into the PP. The existing information (such as already completed clinical trials, competitor overview, claims etc.) may just be in a format not really suitable for the PP. Here you can help the PP team members and speed up the process by providing them with a template for compiling the data. Consider very carefully what data to collect for task and make this work easy for your colleagues. Perhaps a review round before the unpopulated rough template is final and distributed to the PP team could be helpful.

PP template (simple): This could be as simple as one single Excel spread sheet with the publication plan (Chapter 4) on the first page and with each Tab covering the PP supportive tools (Chapter 5). In Figure 4 an Excel template example is provided using the same simple plan used for our example product ActTwoX on the first page. Note that each tab consist of each of the PP tools like CC, Meeting plan etc. As shown in Figure 3, each of the black/grey boxes can be exploded to provide more information of the planned publications or of any gaps. More importantly, before the first PP meeting, each of the tabs in the Excel spread sheet contains information about each of the supportive materials or tasks that need to be populated with data before the PP can actually begin. So the actual plan on the first tab of the Excel spread sheet could be empty or nearly empty before the first PP meeting.

Figure 4. Excel template publication plan - an example with the different PP tools as tabs

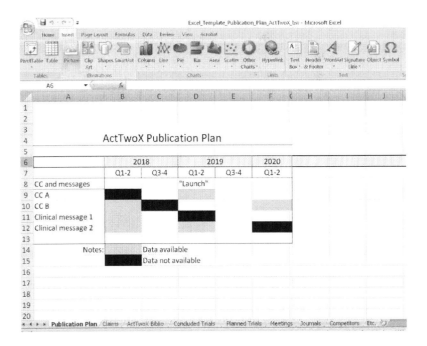

Who to invite: With task definitions on how to complete the PP tools you will get some idea of who will be needed as core members of the PP team and perhaps who could later become ad-hoc members. To make the first meeting successful it would be a good idea to stay with the core team only as this smaller PP team would be more efficient and focused. Depending on where your product is in its life cycle, the core members of the PP team could change. Early in the life cycle MA and R&D could be the core team. Later in the cycle, this team could be expanded to include Clinical and Medical Writing. Ad hoc input and/or participation may be relevant from Biostatistics, Health-Economics, Regulatory, MSL (good competitor insight) and other relevant members of your organization. As mentioned, Marketing should only be allowed on an ad hoc basis for observational/educational purposes and can be a good resource to get an insight into competitors and potential target groups.

Agenda: The first meeting could be a kick-off meeting gathering busy colleagues for an activity where the value is not fully understood but where it is obvious that the preparation is time consuming. So a key to a successful first PP meeting is to get buy-in among the PP team members. Some relevant agenda point for the first meeting could be:

- The plan: Introduction, goals, work outline, meeting frequency, expectations
- Brief introduction to members and roles
- Each member to present supportive material to PP
- PP team feedback: Goal to trim all supportive PP tools to be focused on and to identify "threats"
- The actual planning: What to data to present, what CC to support, and when to publish. Focus on a (for the product) relevant time frame
- Gap analysis: (see below)
- Define work to be performed before next meeting and decide meeting date

The first meeting will be important to create a good team spirit and a productive working culture. It is recommended that this team has enough time to get through a full agenda. PP is an iterative process where the input to the plan can change all the time; clinical trials may not provide the expected data, new competitors enter the playing field etc. The preparation by each member to ensure accuracy and completeness of each of the supporting tasks cannot be emphasized enough. If the quality of this supporting material is good, you will experience an easy PP. Too many "blind spots" will render the planning nearly impossible.

Gap analysis: The intention with the important gap analysis is to identify gaps between the claims you want to support with data (through publications) and the data you actually can achieve at a given time.

This is sometimes a complex analysis as it requires input from several experts in your organization. Sometime data may be available outside your organization (e.g., investigator driven trials). The important thing is to identify IF there is a gap ("black box" in the plan) and to discuss potential ways to fill this gap (pre-clinical trials, clinical trials, design, size, cost, time, etc.). During the first meeting identifying the gaps will be essential and the primary goal. Ways to fill a gap may sometimes require input from departments outside the PP team from Regulatory, Biostatistics, Basic science and more. Regulatory has an important function here: They will know the regulatory strategy of your healthcare products and by involving them in reviewing suggested ways to fill gaps such as through additional clinical trials, Regulatory will be able to identify any potential conflicts with the current regulatory strategy.

The task of suggesting how to fill gaps could be an action point for dedicated members of the team before the next PP meetings. The way a PP team conducts this gap analysis and comes up with solutions to fill identified gaps will define the quality of a PP team.

Updates for next meeting: Keeping the PP tools (bibliography, meeting calendar etc.) up-to-date is critical for the success of the plan. The CC and key clinical messages need to be revised to ensure that they at any time follow the overall product strategy. The bibliographies need to be updated with the latest publications (even if they are not yet published but submitted or accepted for publication) so you can adjust the time lines for the actual publication.

Your company's own clinical trials are obviously essential as they will be the main drivers of your PP; any delays (happening more often than you would actually like....) will have a significant impact on the PP. Competitor publications and planned clinical trials need to be surveyed as this may impact your PP. Meetings should be tracked and especially abstract deadlines are important to be aware of. Journals should be revised at least once a year and the impact factor should be updated according to e.g., Journal Citation Report

(JCR)[6] or similar. This just to give a few examples of some of the updates that are required before the next PP meeting. Last but not least, solutions to fill the gaps (e.g., new clinical trials, systematic reviews, registry data base research etc.) should be investigated and be ready to be presented to the PP team for input.

Meeting frequency: There is usually no need to plan meetings before the updates described above can be completed. This is simply not efficient. The complexity of the PP is often the driver of how often you should meet. In a one product, one indication, early phase (R&D far from launch) you could perhaps consider 2 meetings per year for the PP team. With several indications at time of launch and a lot of data being published, some would consider a meeting every 2 months as beneficial. The meeting frequency will ultimately be defined on how fast your product is being developed and what scientific and clinical data is being generated supporting your healthcare product.

Global needs may require participation from your global affiliates. Video conferencing is an option, but sometimes the PP team will benefit better from in-person meetings to provide improved quality planning. During the start-up phase of a new PP, consider whether an awareness campaign would be beneficial to your project: Inform relevant groups in your organization about the specific PP activities and ongoing needs. Groups like MSL, Marketing & Sales, Licensing, Regulatory, Biostatistics, Scientific laboratories, Manufacturing (especially for medical devices) can profitably be informed about the product PP and the PP teams' specific needs for information. As a small example to illustrate this point, such a presentation given to a sales manager team resulted in very relevant identification and ongoing monitoring of new competitors to be fed back to the PP team. A minor effort to improve the quality of the PP.

CHAPTER 7. ENSURING GOOD PUBLICATION QUALITY

- Good Publication Practice - GPP3
- International Committee of Medical Journal Editors (ICMJE) authorship criteria
- Full transparency – no ghosts
- Other publication guidelines

It must be the goal of any PP team to ensure that all research is published to the highest quality and ethical standards available while respecting legal and regulatory demands. Publications must be accurate, clear, reproducible and unbiased[12] and this should be the primary quality goal for a PP team.

MA has the required scientific and clinical background to ensure that the quality and ethical standards of clinical publications are followed. Good Publication Practice (GPP3)[3] is a well written guideline that is the reference document to any PP team as it states: "Scientific and clinical research should be reported in a complete, accurate, balanced and timely manner"[3]. GPP3 is highly recommended as the preferred guideline to adhere to when drafting your PP. Here are some of the main recommendations that are covered in GPP3[3]:

- Reporting and publication processes should follow applicable laws and guidelines. A good overview of guidelines can be found on the EQUATOR network[13]
- Journal and congress requirements should be followed with focus on ethics, originality and avoidance of duplicate publications
- Planning of scientific and clinical publications requires input from a multidisciplinary team
- Rights, roles, requirements and responsibilities of all contributors (authors and non-authors) should be confirmed a-priori in writing
- Authors must have access to relevant study data
- Authors should take responsibility for how research is presented, published and be part of all stages of publications and presentation development following ICMJE[12]
- Transparency about author and non-author contributions according to ICMJE[12]
- Transparency about sponsors role in design execution, reporting and funding
- All authors and contributors to fully disclose relationships and potential competing interests relating to the research and publication (it is

recommended to use the term "disclosures" over conflicts of interest[3])

The GPP3[3] strongly supports the excellent guidance document published by the ICMJE on its website: www.icmje.org[12]. Here of importance to this book is the guidance to what sometimes becomes a heated discussion point: Who may actually claim authorship to a clinical paper? The ICMJE[12] recommends that authorship should be based on qualification of **ALL** of the following 4 criteria:

1. *Substantial contributions to the conception or design of the work; or the acquisition, analysis, or interpretation of data for the work; AND*
2. *Drafting the work or revising it critically for important intellectual content; AND*
3. *Final approval of the version to be published; AND*
4. *Agreement to be accountable for all aspects of the work in ensuring that questions related to the accuracy or integrity of any part of the work are appropriately investigated and resolved*

Authorship is defined by fulfillment of all of these criteria. However, contributors to a paper that do not fulfill all four criteria should not be on the author list but should still be acknowledged.

Some of the (heated) discussions that can occur around potential authorship can be "cooled down" when using these clear criteria for authorship. Below are two examples on this question: *Can the professor put her/his name on the publication at the end of the work without having participated in the data interpretation, revision of the publication and final approval of the final version to be published ("honorary authorship")?* No – the answer is clear according to the ICMJE authorship criteria. *Can the sponsor clinician who designed the study, participated in conducting the trial and the analyses of the data, co-drafted the manuscript and approved final version of the manuscript and accepted to be accountable for all aspects of the work?* Yes – as this person is fulfilling ALL the four ICMJE authorship criteria. A more correct answer could be: Yes this person should be an author.

One important statement from ICMJE[12] on authorship is that these criteria are not meant for use as of disqualifying authors who otherwise meet the first authorship criteria; all individuals meeting the first criteria should be offered to participate in the review, drafting and final approval.

Beside rules for authorship, ICMJE provides the useful "Recommendations for the Conduct, Reporting, Editing, and Publication of Scholarly Work in Medical Journals" frequently updated at their website: www.icmje.org.

Full transparency is a key aspect of scientific publications. It is a hot topic where the healthcare industry for many years has been suggested to not be fully transparent with the industry driven research. However, this is changing towards the goal of ensuring that all steps in clinical research become fully transparent regardless of whether the research is conducted by academic institutions or the healthcare industry. The process of transparency begins long time (often years) before the actual publication with registration of trial information to clinical trial data bases such as clinicaltrials.gov[10] or EudraCT[11] – an activity specifically required by ICMJE[12]; in fact, registration of clinical trials is a condition of consideration for publication. Note that a "post-hoc" registration is not valid – the trial must be in a registry before the time of first patient enrollment (defined as time of first patient consent)[12]. Too late registration of clinical trials may have the consequence of the editor of a medical journal rejecting your manuscript. This is really a suboptimal situation for the PP.

The publication process (as described above) has also to be fully transparent. This together with the authorship guidelines precludes the use of ghost authorship, i.e., paid authors such as medical writers that write the entire manuscript without being acknowledged for the work. Ghost authorship has been another major critique point against clinical papers published by the healthcare industry, and apparently this phenomenon is still reported even in high impact factor journals[14]. It is important to note that professional medical writing is very helpful and can be done adhering to guidelines ensuring that it is transparent and that the work is acknowledged. Whether a medical writer can qualify as an author is easy to answer by following the ICMJE criteria. For clinical research based on a clinical trial such authorship is rare. However, if a medical writer has conducted a for e.g., systematic review it may be possible that the ICMJE criteria for authorship are fulfilled. In brief: <u>Ghost writing should never occur.</u>

If a "ghost" is used to write a clinical paper someone else must (sometimes) be taking the credit for work not performed i.e., the other side of the medal: The so-called "honorary or gift authors". This issue undermines the credibility and the quality of a scientific publication. In brief: Honorary or gift authorship should never occur.

Transparency is also important with regards to describing who did what in a publication. ICMJE provides good guidance on how to clearly describe who did what in the publication[12].

Disclosures of all information and relevant ties authors may have in the publication and with regards to the research is an essential part of the transparency concept. Disclosures are sometimes seen as something negative or something that potentially downgrades the quality of the scientific work. However, I find disclosures being the right way forward and in no way a minus: The only bad thing is **not to disclose**. Disclosures of actual conflicts of interest such as financial or non-financial support from a sponsor could put scientific judgment at greater risk of introducing bias to a scientific interpretation and conclusion[15]. Such conflicts of interests, however, are part of our daily life and will remain as such unless we introduce a future fully non-for-profit government driven clinical research of ALL drugs, biologics and medical devices with no company involvement. Not likely to happen.

Regulatory authorities are faced with this challenge when assembling expert advisory committees to guide them on evaluating research data from the healthcare industry; the actual clinical experts that conducted the clinical research under evaluation often have some sort of disclosures and ties to the industry. The regulatory authorities would want to have the best experts available in a certain field – and they are the ones with hands-on experience with the actual new healthcare products and most likely have experience from industry sponsored clinical trials. It is inevitable and here it is important to have rules of transparency in place so that disclosures can be known in advance of any counseling. At the time of the acceptance of the final publication many medical journals also require the publication of supplementary materials such as the clinical protocol, the statistical analysis plan, and additional data relevant to the trial. This to ensure transparency and a more indebt understanding of the presented data.

Transparency is an area of a lot of changes. Already now, some scientific journal editors are requesting that independent biostatisticians perform their own tests of the data before publication. Requirements for availability of raw data may be the next steps so that experts can do their own evaluations and re-analyses of the data or perhaps be able to pool data in the future for e.g., in meta-analyses.

Other publication guidelines may be of relevance depending on what type of publication you are preparing to ensure the best quality. Here are just a few of the most relevant ones with the latest versions to be found on the valuable EQUATOR-networks website[13]:

- CONSORT: Reporting of parallel group randomized trials
- STROBE: Reporting of observational studies in epidemiology (cohort, case-control studies, cross-sectional studies)
- PRISMA: Reporting of systematic reviews and meta-analyses
- SRQR: Reporting of qualitative research
- STARD: Reporting of diagnostic accuracy studies
- CHEERS: Economic evaluation reporting standards

The Cochrane Handbook for Systematic Reviews of Interventions is a guideline of the process of preparing a Cochrane systematic review on the effects of healthcare interventions, and it is considered the highest level of guidance in preparing any systematic review[16].

CHAPTER 8. CLINICAL CLAIMS DRIVING THE PLAN

- Clinical claims definition
- Claims process
- Another PP driver

When using the terminology "claims" one is likely to think about Marketing claims. In this book that is neither the case nor the intention. Here we will look at "claims" from a more scientific and clinical point of view and thus will use the terminology "clinical claims" (CC). CC must always be supported by sufficient scientific and clinical evidence.

The CC driven PP suggested in this book is a powerful way of planning what, how and when you publish the clinical data belonging to your healthcare product. It is a very challenging iterative process as you are forced to think backwards from the potential CC to what data need to be generated to support these CC and to the design of the potential clinical trials. Let's take a look at the CC definition and the iterative clinical claims process that could be used in the PP.

Definition: CC can be defined as clinically relevant messages about the healthcare product that say something about the product, typically about its efficacy or safety.

CC process: Initially in your PP process you will need to "begin with the end" in mind. Your product is in the R&D phase and you expect to put it on the market in 5 years from today. Now you should write a mock package insert if it is a drug/biologic or an instruction for use if it is a medical device: As detailed as possible with indication and usage, doses and administration, warnings and precautions, adverse reactions including (mock) data from clinical trials. Make this as close to as possible to the real thing; this has to be realistic and achievable. CC should be clinically relevant and the mock numbers should be something that you could expect coming out of your clinical development program.

Based on you mock "package insert" you can now build efficacy and safety claims that again have to be relevant, realistic and achievable but as understood from this exercise we are only dealing with potential CC; in other words, you may need to adjust (likely to happen) your CC along the way according to data coming out of your clinical trials. Note that some CC may be based on pre-clinical data (like MOA claims) or for medical devices on user data (usability claims). Obviously you will need to have an interaction/sparring between MA and Marketing on defining these CC – they have to be clinical relevant (and achievable) and at the same time have a market relevance (e.g., with regards to competitor situation, consumer impact etc.). Often CC are defined by identified unmet clinical needs in the therapy area of the healthcare product in mind. Marketing has expertise in mapping these unmet clinical needs and should be seen as a good sparring partner and challenger to your clinical claims definitions. It should be emphasized that Marketing (or any other commercial partner) should only provide sparring and that the final definition and selection of CC should be done by MA (or other non-commercial part of your organization).

When you have identified a relevant list of CC that you perhaps have given some sort of ranking into "must have" and "like to have" you can proceed with your PP; for each clinical claim you will need to define what type of clinical (or other) trial would provide you with quality data to support this clinical claim. Trial design, patient characteristics, endpoints, and sample size would be helpful for the PP to determine how realistic it will be to generate data that may support each clinical claim. During this process some CC may have to be re-evaluated and perhaps modified so that eventually quality data can be generated through clinical (or other) trials to support them.

After the CC process described above, you are now ready to add your CC to the PP. The challenge is at this point in time to adhere the CC to a relevant and realistic time line. *When would it be optimal in your products life cycle to have data published for a given clinical claim?*

As an example, some CC can only be supported through the data that comes out of the phase III pivotal trials (the trials that are intended to provide marketing authorization based on conclusive efficacy and safety data). Mechanism of action CC (how the product works perhaps at a receptor level) could be supported much earlier through early pre-clinical or early clinical trials. CC on, for example, long term efficacy may only be available several years after market launch. This just to give an idea of the mapping process.

This process may generate needs for additional CC. One example could be at time of launch where your focus is (for good reasons) on efficacy and safety of your healthcare product. In your PP you may identify the need for data supporting additional health-economic CC – CC that you did not think about in the first place and that due to the clinical trial protocol designs would not be available. The iterative PP process would then trigger a re-evaluation of the relevant clinical trial protocols to include endpoints (variables) that could be sampled and used for health-economic analyses.

Re-evaluation of CC will be natural after the release of data from completed clinical (or other) trials. Here everything is great if you have quality data supporting your intended CC. However, often results of these trials may force you to re-visit your initial CC as data does not support them or only partially support them. In such situations you will need to change the CC and to have a look at you mock package insert/instruction for use to see if this will require an update too. If data does not support your CC, besides changing the CC, additional clinical trials might have to be designed to generate relevant data. Again, the CC process is part of an iterative PP process. In short: CC and clinical data goes "hand in hand".

Other PP driver: Many companies choose to have the PP be driven by scientific questions: You ask the scientific question, design the clinical trial that will answer the question and publish the data.

You could define this as a more "academic" approach. This is a much more forward thinking process and perhaps less iterative as the one suggested in this book. The layout of the plan itself (Figure 4) will still need to include at least some basic information on:

- Study ID
- Publication title
- Journal
- Meeting
- Submission data
- Estimated publication date

This information can be expanded with more details if your product requires that and will substitute the CC driven plan on the first page of the Excel PP shown in Figure 4.

This way of driving the PP is much less time consuming than the CC driven PP. However you will not benefit from the iterative process that the CC driven PP forces you to take. A CC driven PP does not make it less scientific; scientific quality and ethics are the same as if the PP is driven by scientific questions. But you may gain much more by thinking about the CC you wish to support and plan you publications according to these claims. The process forces you to identify gaps in your clinical plans and ways to fill these gaps to maximize the development of your healthcare product.

Regardless of which driver you wish to use (CC or the scientific questions) the supportive material tools described in Chapter 5 (PP tools) are the same. So if you are going to build a plan for the first time begin by generating the supportive materials. You will need an overview of your clinical trials (completed and planned). An overview of past publications will be essential to identify eventual gaps in data availability. Meetings and conference overview will give you a planning tool for targeting the right audience and planning timely presentations of data. And so on. The PP tool activities in Chapter 5 are the "heart" of any PP.

Chapter 9. Planning in Large Companies

- HQ function
- MA as the lead
- Empower the PP team
- Educating the organization
- Outsourcing?

Large companies have the resources to gather a good PP team. Typically the skills of these persons are all there to lift the task of PP. Planning the publications of a healthcare product in any size company is really a headquarter (HQ) function. Its strategic nature and its linking of regulatory (read: What eventually will be a part of the labeling) and R&D/Clinical (read: Data generated from pre-clinical/clinical trials) in the PP process forces this to be a HQ driven effort. PP is time consuming and requires resources taken from a multidisciplinary team with skills such as scientific, clinical, biostatistics, information retrieval, medical writing, regulatory etc. In most companies the only place to find all these skills together is in HQ.

Most of the supportive PP tools (Chapter 5) can be generated without actual physical meetings but the actual challenge of CC and planning of when and where to present data often requires regular face-to-face meetings (see Chapter 6 on PP meetings).

In larger organizations MA has the preferred background to drive the PP. Here the Medical Director should have this role and she/he should pick the relevant PP team members and delegate the needed tasks. To ensure quality and consistency of the PP activities for different products throughout the company it is advisable to have a standard operating procedure (SOP) written on this subject (see Chapter 11).

Introducing PP in larger companies unfamiliar with this strategic task or where the scientific part of the organization typically ("in the past took care of this") took care of this can be a challenge. "Having to take on additional work load to plan publications that previously was taken care of by the R&D department seems like a waste of time". Be prepared for this mindset. You will need to slowly change it through a better understanding of the PP activities and on how your company may benefit from these PP activities. It will be the responsibility for the MA lead to ensure that the team members provides buy-in to this work. But initially, and perhaps more importantly, a top down empowerment of the PP team and its activities from upper management will be critical for the success of the PP team work.

With the PP concept in place the MA lead can begin to increase awareness of the PP to the core departments that will be needed to start this work. Perhaps a brief informational presentation of the concept of PP at the next Regulatory Affairs department meeting or at the next Clinical Development meeting: What is the scope of the PP? Who is involved? Work load in preparing for and attending meetings? What can come out of the PP? Etc. This "awareness road show" should be driven by the core PP team members and has to be repeated and expanded to other parts of the organization. And as soon as the PP team is active and you have results from the planning, this should be shared too.

Education on the PP activities is important also outside HQ and the core PP team. Company affiliates in the different countries may be more sales oriented and less involved in the strategic development of the healthcare products as colleagues working in HQ, however, the country affiliates may have relevant and important input to the different publication plans. Field based colleagues such as MSL's may have knowledge of clinical trials being planned by KOL's. Sales colleagues may have important knowledge of competitor activities that could assist the PP team better in understanding the competitive situation of the healthcare products therapy area.

The following steps will hopefully provide an automatic "flow" of information to your PP team: 1. Empowerment of the PP team from upper management. 2. A companywide SOP on PP activities. 3. A successful awareness campaign on the PP activities provided by the core PP team members to the larger organization: Now MSL's will provide input on clinical trials or new publications to MA. Sales will provide competitor information to Marketing. Country affiliates will provide information of local scientific meetings of importance, etc. Just a few examples of the important flow of information that can reach the PP team and improve its success.

Is there any advantage of outsourcing any of the PP tasks/tools when working in the larger company environment? That will obviously depend on a lot of factors: Actual employee skills, time availability but also taking into consideration the potential costs of outsourcing. Some of the PP tools (described in Chapter 5) are, as mentioned, very time consuming and could be outsourced to vendors that specialize in PP. Some of these vendors have access to large data bases that are up to date on e.g. scientific meetings or target journal information. Your PP team could discuss what tasks would benefit from being outsourced and provide their PP templates to be populated by the vendor on e.g.:

- **Meeting calendar**: The PP team will define to the vendor the scope of what types of meetings are relevant for the PP and have the vendor on a regular basis update all essential information (in the pre-defined PP template) on all relevant meetings/conferences/congresses. And if you also need both to cover international and national meetings some vendors will have the "bandwidth" to do that too.
- **Target journal overview**: Again some vendors have existing data bases on medical and scientific target journals (where your PP will define what the targets are). The vendor can easily provide you with up-to-date information of existing journals but also scan for new relevant journals to your PP.
- **Competitor bibliographies**: Vendors can run searches in literature data bases (Pubmed, Embase, other specialized databases etc.) to ensure that you are always up-to-date on what

is published from your competitors. Furthermore, broad searches can also be used to scan for new competitors. This information can be done on a regular basis and the information be sent to the PP team.

- **Ongoing/new competitor clinical trials**: The vendor can provide output from ongoing searches in clinical trials data bases (like clinicaltrials.gov) on specified competitor product but also on therapy areas so that the PP team has latest information on also new competitor products.

Chapter 10. Planning in Small Companies

- A simple plan
- Resources and lead
- Outsourcing

Small companies may not have all the resources to drive a full plan (neither people nor money). So the first step here is to define how simple you can make the plan. It is worthwhile to have even a simple PP in place than not to have one at all. You are forced to make it simple – but do make it. There is only an upside. We are here talking about a few power point slides where you build the necessary information such as:

- Scope of the PP for your product
- Definitions used in the PP (so that all are on the same page)
- CC and key clinical messages
- A brief plan (as an excel spread sheet, see example in Figure 5) covering:
    - CC to be published
    - Title of publication
    - Data source
    - Planned venue or journal for publication

- o Submission date
- o Planned time for expected publication

Figure 5. Example of the very basic publication plan on a Power Point slide

Publication Plan for ActTwoX

Clinical claim	Title	Data Source	Target Journal	Target Conference	Submission date	Expected time of publication

It does not need to be more complicated than that. You may consider to prepare some of the PP tools as described in Chapter 5 yourself or you could consider to outsource some of this work to a vendor (see below).

This can be done by one person preferably someone from R&D or Clinical if you have no MA yet. As the PP has a highly strategic impact, it is not recommended to outsource the entire ownership of this to a vendor. You may lose the strategic control of this important activity. Another and unfortunately real challenge using vendors is the potential loss of knowhow when the expert in the vendor working on your PP leaves that company. So keep the actual planning in house but consider to have the companies provide you with the important tools needed for generating a good PP. See also Chapter 9 on potential tools that you may benefit from outsourcing.

Outsourcing requires that you "educate" your vendor on the standards and guidelines you wish to follow (e.g. GPP3, ICMJE etc.). These vendors are obviously very professional and have their own SOP's on this topic. Nevertheless, you have your quality criteria in your company that set the high standards for how you wish to conduct your PP. So early education on what standards to adhere to and ongoing monitoring that the standards are being followed is a good idea.

Chapter 11. Publication Planning SOP

- Importance of PP SOP
- Main content
- Training log

In order to ensure good communication and consistent standards used while working with your plans, a well written SOP will be essential and highly recommended. The importance of such a SOP cannot be emphasized enough. The SOP should be crisp and clear and not too lengthy. It should assist the members of the PP team to fully understand the scope and their individual roles and responsibilities while working on the plans. A good SOP will be a valuable training tool that will ensure consistent quality PP conducted throughout the company.

Your company has obviously its own SOP templates and way of writing SOP's, so the following is just some of the basic content that a PP could include:

- **Scope**: Brief and clear scope for the PP activity
- **General definitions**: Definitions similar to the ones used in Chapter 1 so that all PP team members use same terminology
- **PP team definition**: Define the (preferred) lead (MA) and the (preferred) core team members and potential ad hoc members: A cross functional effort
- **Roles and responsibilities**: For each type of member define their roles and responsibilities
- **PP tasks**: The supplementary material tools to the PP that are described in Chapter 5 (PP tools)
- **Quality and ethical guidelines**: Define the guidelines that the PP has to adhere to
- **Sign off procedures**: Who will be required to sign off on PP decisions?

Of importance to the PP SOP is a clarification on the role of the commercial part of the organization in the actual PP process: It is recommended to define a process where the commercial departments (Marketing, Sales etc.) are not actively involved in the PP process in order to adhere to GPP3[3].
It would be critical that such a PP SOP carries the signatures of relevant upper management members to ensure top down empowerment.

This SOP would have to be part of the training log of the core members of the PP team and of any new employees from the relevant parts of the organization. Any significant updates of the SOP would also trigger re-training of the relevant personnel.

Chapter 12. Process and Potential Challenges

- Step by step PP process
- Ongoing planning
- Potential challenges

You should now have a good feeling for the different steps in setting up a PP for your healthcare product. The step by step process outlined in this book is just meant as a template to stimulate your imagination as you will most likely modify the template to better serve your specific needs. It is easy to overdo the PP and make it too cumbersome – so try to limit your publication plan to something that is acceptable for your organization.

In the ongoing PP it will be important to "keep up the steam". You will need to ensure that the PP team delivers the updated PP tools and that they will all attend the PP meetings. In the ideal world the publication plan will at some time achieve only "grey" boxes meaning that you have no gaps for each CC. That seems too good to be true – and it often is. You could set some performance targets that are ambitious but achievable for the PP team to keep their attention to the tasks in the ongoing planning process.

Expect that your PP team will meet some challenges in the ongoing PP process. Here are some that could occur but several others are to be expected in this complex process:

Pivotal trial does not meet primary endpoint: That is a big one as it definitely impacts the CC supporting your healthcare product and it impacts whether the product can (ever) reach the market. The PP team can here become a strategic support to the management team in your company as you have already anticipated this outcome and as you have a deep understanding of the clinical data supporting the trial. Missing the primary endpoint raises a lot of questions regarding design of the clinical trial: Was the patient group included in the study correctly defined? Was the allocated treatments regimen relevant and optimal? Did a sub-group seem to benefit better? Did the trial identify any risks to the patients that could change the risk benefit assessment? And many more such questions. The PP team should be involved in these important discussions that could lead to a revised development strategy of the healthcare product.

The data is not available to the right time:
Frustrating reality of conducting clinical trials: They are hard to plan according to a well defined timeline. So when the data is not available for publication this directly affects the publication plan. In your ongoing process you will need to take this into consideration and have contingency plans. It is likely to happen to any PP teams and you just have to be ready for this.

Loss of knowhow: PP teams consist of people and people tend to move on. This creates (not only for PP) a loss of knowhow with the risk of losing the strategic focus of the PP for your specific product. SOP's and training can help standardizing the quality of the PP in case of a change in personnel. Furthermore, making the plan self-explanatory is a good investment: You should as a newcomer be able to read the document (e.g., the Excel spreadsheet suggested in Figure 4) and understand the strategic scope of the plan. So a little informational text will go a long way to assist future new members of the PP team.

You will most likely identify many more interesting challenges. The key to success here is to have a good PP team in place: PP is a teamwork.

Strive for excellence in your PP!

CHAPTER 13. LINKS TO PUBLICATION WEBSITES

The International Society for Medical Publication Professionals (ISMPP) to find latest edition of Good Publication Practice (GPP3): www.ismpp.org/gpp3

International Committee of Medical Journal Editors (ICMJE) to find latest author ship criteria and recommendation for publications in medical journals: www.icmje.org

The EQUATOR Network website and database to find a remarkable overview of the latest versions of reporting guidelines based on study types (e.g., CONSORT, STROBE, PRISMA and many more) www.equator-network.org

FDA Guidance for Industry: Distributing Scientific and Medical Publications on Unapproved New Uses — Recommended Practices. To get the regulatory perspective on unapproved new uses: www.fda.gov/downloads/drugs/guidancecompliancereg ulatoryinformation/guidances/ucm387652.pdf

Global Medical Writers organizations (US/EU). To get access to latest medical writing know how: www.amwa.org and www.emwa.org

Committee on publication ethics (COPE). To access official guidelines and official standards on publications and ethics: www.publicationethics.org

Examples of publication plan vendors: Vendors that may provide you with some of the PP tools if you wish to outsource. Note that there are many (good) vendors on the market so use the time to find the perfect fit:
http://www.aspire-scientific.com/,
https://www.parexel.com/,
http://www.envisionpharmagroup.com/,
http://www.insciencecommunications.com/,
http://www.cactusglobal.com/

and many many more.

ABOUT THE AUTHOR

Author's vision: *To bring the best treatments to the patients – as fast as possible.*

Peter Kruse, MD, PhD, is an independent clinical consultant based in Europe with a total of 17+ years experience with the Pharmaceutical and Medical Device industry. Dr. Kruse delivers professional medical, clinical, and scientific advice and support to Pharmaceutical and Medical Device companies, Academic Institutions and Investment firms. Dr. Kruse has an special interest in building MA teams and provides education on the subject. Dr. Kruse is also coaching individuals in the healthcare industry and assist in their career planning.

Prior to working as an independent clinical consultant, Dr. Kruse worked in the Pharmaceutical and in the Medical Device Industry: Global strategic marketing, medical affairs and global clinical development at Novo Nordisk in Europe and the US. His main responsibilities were the support and development of recombinant activated Factor VII as a haemostatic agent into surgery related indications. Dr. Kruse led a global development team that conducted clinical development in surgery. In Baxter BioSurgery, Dr. Kruse was the head of US Medical Affairs, supporting the pipe-line of haemostatic devices and biologics used in surgery, devices for anti adhesion and novel treatments for wound management. He has experience in the creation and expansion of several medical affairs departments.

Dr. Kruse received both his medical degree (MD) and PhD from University of Copenhagen, Denmark. He worked 12+ years as a physician at university hospitals in Copenhagen where he trained in general surgery (GI-, cardiothoracic-, urologic-, and orthopedic surgery) and intensive care. His publications are in physiology, gastroenterology and surgery.

Dr. Kruse has management experience from leading medical affairs teams, global clinical development teams and several university based surgery teams. He has been an officer and a physician in the Danish Navy. Dr. Kruse has done business training through Medical Product Executive Diploma Program at Scandinavian International Management Institute and management courses including an executive course at Harvard Business School. Furthermore, Dr. Kruse has extensive drug development training from PERI, Brookwood, DIA and others.

Other books by Dr. Kruse in the *Healthcare Industry Excellence* Series:

1. Want a Career in the Healthcare Industry?
   www.createspace.com/6060076
   This provides a brief overview of the Healthcare Industry for Healthcare professionals that are aiming at a new career in a Pharmaceutical or Medical device company.
2. Medical Affairs in the Healthcare Industry: An introduction
   www.createspace.com/5909257
   This focuses on the specialty Medical Affairs as a key role in the Healthcare Industry and to give a brief overview of the Medical Affairs skills.

More about Dr. Kruse please visit the website: www.webalice.it/morarokruse/ where you will also be able to contact him.

REFERENCES

[1] Kruse P. Medical Affairs in the Healthcare Industry - An Introduction. Createspace: https://www.createspace.com/5909257, 2015.

[2] Fugh-Berman A, Dodgson SJ. Ethical considerations of publication planning in the pharmaceutical industry. Open Med 2008;2(4):e121-e124.

[3] Battisti WP, Wager E, Baltzer L, Bridges D, Cairns A, Carswell CI, et al. Good Publication Practice for Communicating Company-Sponsored Medical Research: GPP3. Ann Intern Med 2015;163(6):461-464.

[4] Wikipedia. List of largest pharmaceutical settlements. Website 2017 February 2Available from: URL: www.en.wikipedia.org/wiki/List_of_largest_pharmaceutical_settlements

[5] Rawlins M. Reflections: NICE, health economics, and outcomes research. Value Health 2012;15(3):568-569.

[6] Thompson Reuters. Journal Citation Reports (JCR). Website 2017 February 2Available from: URL: http://about.jcr.incites.thomsonreuters.com/

[7] National Library of Medicine N. PubMed. Website 2015Available from: URL: http://www.ncbi.nlm.nih.gov/pubmed

[8] Elsevier. Embase. Website 2015Available from: URL: https://www.elsevier.com/solutions/embase-biomedical-research

[9] Cochrane. Cochrane Library. Website 2017 February 2Available from: URL: http://www.cochranelibrary.com/

[10] U.S.National Institutes of Health. ClinicalTrials.gov (US). Website 2017 February 2Available from: URL: https://www.clinicaltrials.gov/

[11] European Medicines Agency (EMA). EU Clinical Trials Register (EU CTR). Website 2017 February 2Available from: URL: https://www.clinicaltrialsregister.eu/ctr-search/search

[12] ICMJE. ICMJE authorship criteria. Website 2017 February 2Available from: URL: http://www.icmje.org/recommendations/browse/roles-and-responsibilities/defining-the-role-of-authors-and-contributors.html

[13] EQUATOR. Enhancing the QUAlity and Transparency Of health Research - EQUATOR. Website 2017 February 2Available from: URL: http://www.equator-network.org/

[14] Wislar JS, Flanagin A, Fontanarosa PB, Deangelis CD. Honorary and ghost authorship in high impact biomedical journals: a cross sectional survey. BMJ 2011;343:d6128.

[15] Lundh A, Sismondo S, Lexchin J, Busuioc OA, Bero L. Industry sponsorship and research outcome. Cochrane Database Syst Rev 2012;12:MR000033.

[16] Cochrane. Cochrane Handbook for Systematic Reviews of Interventions. Website 2017 February 2Available from: URL: http://training.cochrane.org/handbook

Made in the USA
Columbia, SC
05 January 2021

30368900R00057